DATE DUE

OFFICIALLY
WITHDRAWN

AUG   2007

DK READERS

Level 3

Spacebusters: The Race to the Moon
Beastly Tales
Shark Attack!
Titanic
Invaders from Outer Space
Movie Magic
Plants Bite Back!
Time Traveler
Bermuda Triangle
Tiger Tales
Aladdin
Heidi
Zeppelin: The Age of the Airship
Spies
Terror on the Amazon
Disasters at Sea
The Story of Anne Frank
Abraham Lincoln: Lawyer, Leader, Legend
George Washington: Soldier, Hero,
    President
Extreme Sports

Spiders' Secrets
The Big Dinosaur Dig
Space Heroes: Amazing Astronauts
The Story of Chocolate
School Days Around the World
NFL: Whiz Kid Quarterbacks
MLB: Home Run Heroes: Big Mac,
    Sammy, and Junior
MLB: World Series Heroes
MLB: Record Breakers
MLB: Down to the Wire: Baseball's Great
    Pennant Races
Star Wars: Star Pilot
The X-Men School
Abraham Lincoln: Abogado, Líder,
    Leyenda en español
Fantastic Four: The World's Greatest
    Superteam
Star Wars: I want to be a Jedi
Polar Bear Alert!

Level 4

Days of the Knights
Volcanoes and Other Natural Disasters
Secrets of the Mummies
Pirates! Raiders of the High Seas
Horse Heroes
Trojan Horse
Micro Monsters
Going for Gold!
Extreme Machines
Flying Ace: The Story of Amelia Earhart
Robin Hood
Black Beauty
Free at Last! The Story of
    Martin Luther King, Jr.
Joan of Arc
Spooky Spinechillers
Welcome to The Globe! The
    Story of Shakespeare's Theater
Antarctic Adventure
Space Station: Accident on Mir
Atlantis: The Lost City?
Dinosaur Detectives
Danger on the Mountain: Scaling
    the World's Highest Peaks
Crime Busters
The Story of Muhammad Ali
First Flight: The Story of the
    Wright Brothers
D-Day Landings: the Story of
    the Allied Invasion
Solo Sailing
NFL: NFL's Greatest Upsets
NFL: Rumbling Running Backs
NFL: Super Bowl!

MLB: Strikeout Kings
MLB: Super Shortstops: Jeter,
    Nomar, and A-Rod
MLB: The Story of the New York Yankees
MLB: The World of Baseball
MLB: October Magic: All the Best
    World Series!
WCW: Feel the Sting
WCW: Going for Goldberg
JLA: Batman's Guide to Crime
    and Detection
JLA: Superman's Guide to the Universe
JLA: Aquaman's Guide to the Oceans
JLA: Wonder Woman's Book of Myths
JLA: Flash's Guide to Speed
JLA: Green Lantern's Guide to
    Great Inventions
The Story of the X-Men: How it all Began
Creating the X-Men: How Comic
    Books Come to Life
Spider-Man's Amazing Powers
The Story of Spider-Man
The Incredible Hulk's Book of Strength
The Story of the Incredible Hulk
Transformers: The Awakening
Transformers: The Quest
Transformers: The Unicron Battles
Transformers: The Uprising
Transformers: Megatron Returns
Transformers: Terracon Attack
Star Wars: Galactic Crisis!
Fantastic Four: Evil Adversaries
Dinosaurs! Battle of the Bones

A Note to Parents

DK READERS is a compelling program for beginning readers, designed in conjunction with leading literacy experts, including Dr. Linda Gambrell, Professor of Education at Clemson University. Dr. Gambrell has served as President of the National Reading Conference and the College Reading Association, and has recently been elected to serve as President of the International Reading Association.

Beautiful illustrations and superb full-color photographs combine with engaging, easy-to-read stories to offer a fresh approach to each subject in the series. Each DK READER is guaranteed to capture a child's interest while developing his or her reading skills, general knowledge, and love of reading.

The five levels of DK READERS are aimed at different reading abilities, enabling you to choose the books that are exactly right for your child:

Pre-level 1: Learning to read
Level 1: Beginning to read
Level 2: Beginning to read alone
Level 3: Reading alone
Level 4: Proficient readers

The "normal" age at which a child begins to read can be anywhere from three to eight years old. Adult participation through the lower levels is very helpful for providing encouragement, discussing storylines, and sounding out unfamiliar words.

No matter which level you select, you can be sure that you are helping your child learn to read, then read to learn!

LONDON, NEW YORK, MUNICH,
MELBOURNE, AND DELHI

Editor Julia Roles
U.S. Editor John Searcy
Production Georgina Hayworth

Reading Consultant
Linda Gambrell, Ph.D.

Produced by
Shoreline Publishing Group LLC
Editorial Director James Buckley, Jr.
Designer Tom Carling, carlingdesign.com

First American Edition, 2007
Published in the United States by DK Publishing
375 Hudson Street, New York, New York 10014

Copyright © 2007 Dorling Kindersley Limited

Dorling Kindersley is represented in Canada by
Tourmaline Editions Inc
662 King Street West, Suite 304
Toronto, Ontario M5V 1M7

DK books are available at special discounts when purchased in bulk
for sales promotions, premiums, fund-raising, or educational use.
For details, contact: DK Publishing Special Markets, 375 Hudson
Street, New York, New York 10014, or SpecialSales@dk.com

A catalog record for this book
is available from the Library of Congress.

ISBN: 978-0-7566-3140-6 (Paperback)
ISBN: 978-0-7566-3143-7 (Hardcover)

Color reproduction by Colourscan, Singapore
Printed and bound in China by L. Rex Printing Co., Ltd

07 08 09 10 11 10 9 8 7 6 5 4 3 2 1

The publisher would like to thank the following for their kind
permission to reproduce their photographs:
(b=below; t=top)
AGE Fotostock: 4, 28; Corbis: 3, 10, 14b, 16, 26, 30, 42, 46;
Daybreak Photography: 27t; Dreamstime.com: 9, 31, 37, 38, 45;
Getty Images: 19, 23, 25, 32, 34, 35, 39, 44; iStock: 8; Juniors
Bildarchiv: 12; Minden Pictures: 40; Photos.com: 6, 13, 15, 20, 21,
24, 27b, 43; Julia Roles: 5, 14t, 18.

All other images copyright © Dorling Kindersley
For more information see: www.dkimages.com

Discover more at
www.dk.com

Contents

Danger ahead!   4

Step by step   8

Polar bear town   14

Polar bear "jail"   18

At Hudson Bay   22

Life on the ice   24

Mother and cubs   28

Hot and hungry   38

New threat   42

The future   46

Glossary   48

 **READERS**

READING
3
ALONE

Polar Bear Alert!

Written by Debora Pearson

DK Publishing

Danger ahead!

Be careful. Be VERY careful. It's not safe to be here, outside the town of Churchill, Manitoba, during the fall.

Churchill is in Canada's far north and fall can be a bone-chilling season in this part of the world. The temperature drops well below freezing. Icy winds blast across the permanently frozen ground, called tundra. Fresh snow covers the entire landscape.

Right now, hundreds of animals are on the move here. Every fall, they travel across the tundra to the frozen waters of Hudson Bay. These creatures must reach their destination—or they will starve to death.

One of them has left fresh tracks close by. Each footprint is the size of a dinner plate and has five sturdy claw marks. What has made these enormous footprints and where exactly is this creature heading?

The world's largest land carnivore, a polar bear, is just ahead. This one is an adult male and he's ravenous.

For the past four months, this bear has eaten only a few berries and birds' eggs. He and the other polar bears in this region hunt for their main food only when ice covers Hudson Bay—from late fall to early summer. Then the bears stay on the ice and catch ringed seals. When the ice breaks up in early summer, the bears must return to land where there is little food for them.

Polar bear places
There are about 25,000 polar bears worldwide. They all live in and around the Arctic. About two-thirds of them are in Canada.

The Arctic

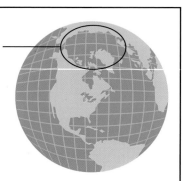

Step by step

The bear's journey began just west of Wapusk National Park, 30 miles (45 km) east of Churchill. Wapusk Park is a protected area of wilderness where many polar bears spend the summer. During the winter, female polar bears build their dens and give birth to their cubs there.

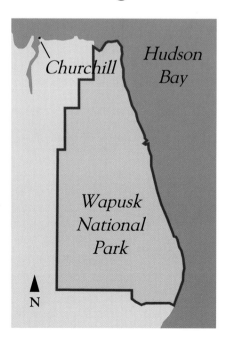

Churchill

Hudson Bay

Wapusk National Park

N

The male bear arrived near Wapusk Park last July. He was carried here on a chunk of melting ice that swept him to the coast close to the park. He has

spent all his time near the shore since then, waiting for fall and listening to the noisy seabirds that flap overhead.

The water near Wapusk Park freezes later than the water near Churchill. Once the days grow shorter and the temperature drops, the bear heads toward Churchill. As he walks, he sees a familiar sight.

A tundra vehicle growls over the snow and stops in the distance. Its huge tires spread its weight across the snow so that it doesn't leave deep tracks behind. It contains tourists from around the world who are here bear-watching.

Some polar bears avoid tundra vehicles, but not the big bear. He wanders over to it and stands on his hind legs for a better look. What's inside this one?

The bear towers 9 feet (2.7 m) in the air, just high enough to reach the vehicle's windows. He spots a girl's face on the other side of the glass. The bear and the girl each stare at the strange creature before them. Finally, his curiosity satisfied, the bear continues on his way.

As the big bear plods along, he stretches his neck and sniffs the air. Like all polar bears, he has a keen sense of smell. He can detect seals up to half a mile (1 km) away. With his nose alone, he can tell that a fast-moving Arctic hare has recently been here.

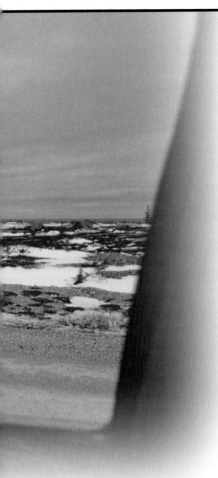

The bear sniffs again and picks up the smell of car exhaust. After a while, a car zooms past him, heading the way he is going. He's very close to the town of Churchill and that means he's almost at the end of his journey. Just beyond Churchill is the place on Hudson Bay where the sea ice forms first in the fall.

Soon the bear will find the food he urgently needs. But first, he must get past the town.

Arctic hare

Polar bear town

Churchill, "The Polar Bear Capital of the World," is a small town with its own schools, public library, stores, restaurants, hotels, and port.

In winter, this remote community can be reached only by train or airplane. In summer, when the bay isn't frozen, it can also be reached by ship. The only

Big bear name
The Inuit call the polar bear "Nanuq" in their native language of Inuktitut. This is a stone carving of Nanuq.

road out of Churchill goes just a short distance along the coast of Hudson Bay.

The town lies on land where people and polar bears have lived for centuries. Native people, such as the Inuit, Cree, and Dene, were already here when the first Europeans arrived almost 400 years ago. Polar bears were here, too. In the fall of 1619, Jens Munk, the Danish explorer who discovered the Churchill area, wrote in his journal about his encounter here with a "large white bear."

Something special is happening
in Churchill tonight. It's the last day
of October—Halloween. Children in
costumes are running door-to-door and
calling out, "Trick or treat!"

Halloween happens during bear

season so everyone here must be extra careful. On the day of Halloween, a helicopter flies over the town to check for bears in the area. On Halloween night, fire trucks, ambulances, and volunteers patrol the streets.

A bear control zone around Churchill also helps people stay safe at all times. A team of wildlife officers from the Polar Bear Alert Program guards the control zone and prevents hungry bears from reaching the town. This is especially important for children and their parents on Halloween.

Suddenly, an officer spots the male bear. Is the bear about to enter the control zone?

Polar bear "jail"

The wildlife officers watch the intruder carefully.

If the bear comes closer, they will try to drive it away by flashing bright lights and making loud noises. If that doesn't work, they may have to put it in polar bear "jail."

Polar Bear Compound

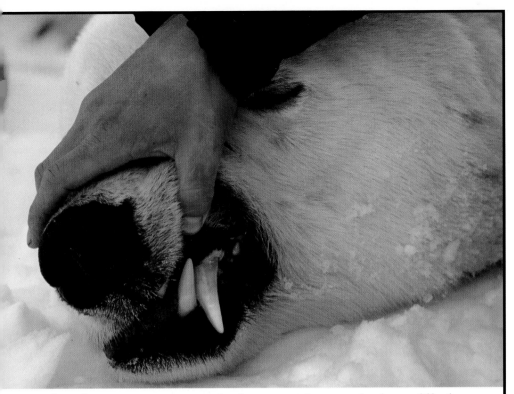

Before bears are captured, they are shot with drug-filled darts that temporarily stop them from moving.

The bear jail's real name is "Polar Bear Compound." It's a building with 28 bear pens on the edge of Churchill. The bears are not fed while they're locked up so they don't get used to food from humans. After Hudson Bay freezes, all the bears are released on the ice so they can hunt for their own food.

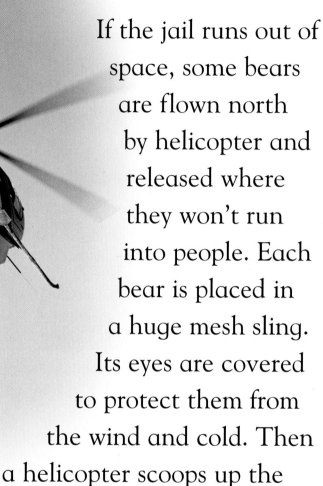

If the jail runs out of space, some bears are flown north by helicopter and released where they won't run into people. Each bear is placed in a huge mesh sling. Its eyes are covered to protect them from the wind and cold. Then a helicopter scoops up the bear and carries it to its new home, away from Churchill.

Outside town, the male bear paces nervously in the snow. Should he go closer to this strange place? Perhaps he will find something to eat there.

The bear doesn't know that polar bears aren't allowed in town. He's growing hungrier all the time, but he senses that it's not safe for him to go through Churchill. He begins walking, staying well away from the town.

At Hudson Bay

By the time the male bear reaches Hudson Bay, just beyond Churchill, other polar bears are already here. They are all waiting for freeze-up, when ice covers Hudson Bay.

The ice begins to form solidly near the shore, but the bears know that further out the ice will form first as pancake ice (pieces of ice separated by water). They constantly test the ice, hoping that it will soon be strong enough to hold them. Sometimes they crash into the water, but polar bears are excellent swimmers and they are back on land or solid ice in no time.

The bears' wait continues. Then one night in late November, a storm blows in and the temperature drops.

The next day, after the storm, the ice seems to stretch all the way to the horizon. Freeze-up has come.

Life on the ice

For the next eight months, during the coldest time of the year, the ice-covered bay will be the polar bear's home.

How does the big bear survive here for so long? Like all polar bears, he has a body that is suited for life on the ice. Its unique features, or adaptations, help keep him warm.

One important feature is his coat of fur. It has two layers. An outer layer of

glossy hairs sheds snow, ice, and water.
Underneath, a dense layer of fur traps
heat from the bear's body and prevents
it from escaping. A layer of fat under his
skin also protects him from the cold. An
adult bear's
layer of fat
can be as
thick as a
down-filled
quilt.

To find food, the bear roams the ice in search of a ringed seal's breathing hole. Then he waits there for the seal to surface from the water below.

The ice is slippery but the big bear moves across it without sliding. The pads of his feet have small bumps and hairs that help him grip the ice. Indentations on the bear's footpads act like suction cups and keep him from slipping.

When the bay is ice free, ringed seals sometimes lie on the rocks. But not for long if there's a polar bear nearby.

Life on the ice is difficult for the bear, even with his unique adaptations. It can take many attempts for him to catch a single seal.

Barely there

While hunting, a polar bear must remain completely still by a seal's breathing hole. Sometimes the wait is so long the bear falls asleep!

Mother and cubs

Some polar bears aren't out on the frozen bay. More than 100 female bears are still on land, in Wapusk National Park. They're getting ready for the birth of their cubs.

A polar bear's cubs are born in November or December. In the fall, instead of going out on the ice to hunt and feed, the female bear builds a den where she will give birth and nurse her cubs. Choosing a good location for her den is important. She heads inland, away from the flat coast, and looks for low sloping land that will be covered by drifting snow. Then she digs her den. It is about as long and wide as a single bed and about 3 feet (1 m) high.

One night in December, as the northern lights shimmer across the sky, twin bear cubs are born.

It's -20°F (-29°C) outside, but it's cozy and comfortable inside the den. Heat from the mother's body keeps all

the bears warm, while a blanket of snow over the den holds in the heat.

The newborn twins are tiny and helpless. Each cub weighs less than 2 pounds (1 kg) and its eyes are closed at birth. For the next three months, the cubs will remain here while their mother cuddles them and nurses them with her rich milk. The three bears will stay together for more than two years. During this time, the cubs will learn all about life as a polar bear in the Arctic.

By early March, each cub weighs
ten times as much as it did at birth.
Their mother, however, is steadily losing

weight. When she was pregnant she gained about 440 pounds (200 kg) of fat. But she hasn't eaten for eight months and, during that time, she has been living off the stored-up fat in her body. She must eat soon or she will become too weak to care for her cubs. First, she must break out of the snow-covered den.

The cubs have spent their entire lives inside this cozy shelter, so it's a shock when their mother claws through the snow to create an opening. She protects them from the cold air as they take their first peek at the strange white world outside. The twins don't know it, but their mother will soon lead them on a long journey to Hudson Bay. The mother bear will hunt and eat seals there.

The curious cubs follow their mother outside. There is so much to see and do here! The cubs jump and run and roll around, scattering snow everywhere. As they spend time playing in the snow and nursing outdoors, they gradually get accustomed to the intense cold.

One week after emerging from the den, the cubs are ready to make the trip with their mother to the coast of Hudson Bay. The mother bear is eager to reach the ice and find food, but she doesn't rush her cubs. The bears stop often along the way to rest and nurse. Sometimes, when the snow is very deep, the mother lets one of the cubs climb onto her back and ride instead of walk.

The mother bear and her cubs walk out onto the frozen bay at the edge of Wapusk Park. Finally, it's time for the mother to eat. While she searches for seals, she keeps her cubs close by. They get their first hunting lessons by watching their mother in action. If the cubs get restless and start to wander off, she calls them back with a low growl.

All the bears remain on Hudson Bay until July, when the ice melts and breaks up. As the ice begins to melt, the seals slip away in the open water and it becomes too difficult for the bears to catch them. The bears float back to land on chunks of ice. Their hunting season is over. It will be a long time before the polar bears of Hudson Bay eat seals again.

Hot and hungry

In summer, the temperature sometimes rises to 90°F (33°C). This time of year can be hot and unpleasant for a polar bear. Its body is adapted for winter weather, when it needs protection from the severe cold. In warm weather, a bear's heavy coat of fur and layer of fat can cause it to overheat. It must stay cool—but how?

All polar bears like to swim. One way they stay cool is by swimming short distances in Hudson Bay's cold waters. Their fat helps them float and they use their huge paws like oars to move smoothly through the water. Polar bears also have an extra set of transparent eyelids that act like goggles and protect their eyes while they're underwater. When the bears leave the water, they shake themselves off like dogs.

During summer and early fall, a polar bear must live for months without food. Many animals will die if they can't eat for long periods—but not the polar bear.

A polar bear has a unique way of adapting to times when it has nothing to eat. After seven to ten days without food, the bear's metabolism (the way it uses the energy in food) slows down. Its

body temperature drops slightly and its heart beats more slowly. The bear uses less energy than it did before. It spends most of its time resting and staying still.

When the bear has a steady supply of food again, its metabolism speeds up. Then the bear uses more energy and becomes much more active. It spends more of its time swimming and walking.

New threat

The polar bears of Churchill must overcome bitter cold, hunger, and intense heat to survive. Today, they face a new threat: global warming. Global warming is the gradual rise in the surface temperature of the earth. One of its main causes is the buildup of greenhouse gases in the atmosphere.

Warmer temperatures cause the ice on

Hudson Bay to thaw earlier in the spring
and freeze later in the fall. When this
happens, the bears have less time to hunt
and eat. They return to land without
gaining all the weight they need.

Greenhouse gases

Greenhouse gases are released
into the air when people burn
fossil fuels such as gasoline to
run cars and other machines.

Because their hunting season on the ice is getting shorter, polar bears must look for some of their food elsewhere—often in the town of Churchill. This can lead to more encounters between people and bears—a dangerous situation!

When it comes to the problem of global warming, there is no single solution. But everyone can help by using energy wisely. When people drive cars, the cars burn fossil fuels. When people take the bus or train or share rides with friends, less fuel is burned. When people ride bicycles, the bicycles don't use any fossil fuels so no harmful greenhouse gases are released into the air.

The future

When fall comes, the male bear, the mother and her cubs, and many other polar bears will head to the ice once again. Is time running out for them? Will their annual journey to Hudson Bay eventually become a thing of the past? Or will these bears and the ones that are born after them continue to roam here for years to come?

Many scientists believe that polar bears everywhere face an uncertain future. Their habitat is changing in ways that people have not seen before. Will polar bears adapt to these

changes? No one knows exactly what
will happen.

Life has always been challenging for
polar bears. Now they face even greater
challenges. Can you think of ways
that humans can help make sure these
magnificent creatures survive?

Glossary

Atmosphere
The layer of gases that surrounds the earth.

Attempts
Efforts to do something.

Bear pens
Closed-in areas for holding polar bears until they are released on the ice. Each pen holds one polar bear.

Bear season
The time during the fall when bears gather near the town of Churchill and wait for Hudson Bay to freeze.

Carnivore
An animal that eats mainly meat.

Destination
The place at the end of a journey.

Detect
To discover or notice.

Encounter
A meeting, especially one that is not planned ahead of time.

Habitat
The natural home of an animal or plant, where it lives and grows.

Horizon
The line where the sky and the earth appear to meet.

Indentation
A pushed-in surface or a dent.

Nurse
The way a female mammal feeds her young, using milk made by her own body.

Port
A place by an ocean, river, lake, or sea where ships can load and unload their cargo.

Pregnant
The term used to describe a female who is carrying her young inside her body, before she gives birth.

Ravenous
Extremely hungry.

Remote
Located out of the way, far from other people.

Tundra
Large, open areas in the Arctic where the soil is frozen and no trees grow.

Tundra vehicle
A giant bus-like vehicle that carries people across the tundra and lets them safely see polar bears up close.

Unique
One of a kind.

Index

adaptations 24, 25, 26, 27, 40
Arctic 7, 31
  hare 13

bear control zone 17
bear season 17
bear-watching 11
breathing hole 26, 27

Canada 4
carnivore 7
children 16, 17
Churchill 4, 8, 9, 13, 14, 15, 16, 17, 19, 20, 21, 22, 44
coast 8, 15, 29, 35
compound, polar bear 19
Cree 15
cubs 28, 30, 31, 33, 34, 35, 36, 46

darts, drug-filled 19
Dene 15
den 8, 28, 29, 30, 31, 33, 35

Europeans 15
eyes 20, 31, 39

fall 4, 7, 9, 28, 40, 46
fat 25, 33, 38, 39

feet/paws 26, 39
food 7, 13, 19, 26, 35, 40, 41, 44
footprints 4, 5
freeze-up 22, 23
fuels, fossil 43, 45
fur 24, 25, 38

gases, greenhouse 42, 43, 45
global warming 42, 45

Halloween 16, 17
helicopter 17, 20
Hudson Bay 4, 7, 13, 15, 17, 19, 22, 33, 35, 36, 39, 43, 46
hunting 27, 33, 36, 44

ice 7, 8, 13, 19, 22, 23, 24, 25, 26, 27, 28, 35, 36, 43, 46
  pancake 22
Inuktitut 15
Inuit 15

jail, polar bear 18, 19, 20

Manitoba, 4
metabolism 40, 41
Munk, Jens 15

Nanuq 15
northern lights 30, 31

officers, wildlife 17, 18

people/humans 11, 15, 16, 17, 44, 45, 46
Polar Bear Alert Program 17

seabirds 9
seals 7, 12, 26, 27, 33, 36
smell, sense of 12
snow 4, 11, 20, 25, 29, 31, 33, 34, 35
swimming 39, 41
summer 7, 8, 38, 40

tires 11
tourists 11
tracks 4, 11
tundra 4
  vehicle 11

Wapusk National Park 8, 28, 36
wilderness 8
winter 8, 38